"It jabs the conscience, pokes at the heart, and alternately touches nerves of deep human concern and lighter human humor. Funny, it is often very, very moving."

—Malcolm Boyd

FUNNY, YOU DON'T LOOK CHRISTIAN

by Robert M. Herhold

with an afterword by
William Robert Miller

ILLUSTRATIONS BY ROY DOTY

WEYBRIGHT AND TALLEY
New York

TO MURIEL

who doesn't have to look Christian

Introduction

The two most striking structures in Cologne, Germany, are a magnificent cathedral and a daring suspension bridge.

The cathedral, begun in the thirteenth century, is a labor of love. Its twin spires are like giant fingers pointing to God in heaven. The interior and exterior are bedecked with ornate statues and symbols. One deutsch mark purchases admission to the cathedral's treasury with its gold caskets generously sprinkled with jewels. There are enough gold crosses, tabernacles and bishop's crooks, all loaded with precious stones, to make the down payment on another cathedral. The claim that the Three Wise Men are buried in the cathedral is a tourist attraction not unlike Boothill Cemetery in Tombstone, Arizona. Throngs jabber and gawk their way through the cathedral's nave, while a handful kneel in prayer. Most people show about the same reverence for the cathedral that they do for the railroad station across the street.

The bridge is a spidery span, flung defiantly across the Rhine. Unlike the cathedral, its purpose is unmistakably clear. It supports crunching traffic without an excess ounce in its structure. Built after World War II, its A frame cantilever arch and twelve cables are an engineering marvel. The simplicity of the bridge is in marked contrast to the cluttered gothic of the cathedral. Engineers, artists and newsboys all marvel at the functional beauty of the Severinsbrucke.

The cathedral represents traditional religion. It exhibits bold, outward authority, but people inside are chewing gum and buying postcards. For most people the spires point in the direction of the next space shot rather than to God. The cathedral presupposes a medieval world view and social order. Few people believe that God dwells where the spires point—or if he does, that's probably as good a place for him as any. His reality and relevance are as obscure as the identity of the saints backed against the walls of the cathedral. A society in which the word of God or the authority of the church is supreme no longer exists. Man, not God, is the measure of all things. Customs like grace at meals or the family attending church together are the exception, not the rule. In the words of Dietrich Bonhoeffer, we live in a "world come of age." God has been technologically unemployed. Mathematics has elbowed theology off the throne as the queen of the sciences.

The bridge is a much better religious symbol for most people than the cathedral. The bridge is functional, uncluttered and contemporary. The architect of the bridge did not begin by asking what a bridge should look like, but what a bridge should do. He designed a structure to support people and vehicles as they traveled from one side of the Rhine to the other. And he did this with such audacious simplicity that the bridge is a thing of beauty. Because it is functional and uncluttered, it appeals to us. The bridge speaks to a generation for whom mystery, sentimentality and excess baggage are taboo. We would like a religious faith with the fresh, clean lines of the bridge.

The bridge is contemporary. It was designed for a particular time—today and the foreseeable future. It was built for modern traffic, not for horses and carts. The designer dared to be untraditional, while not ignoring certain fundamentals of engineering. Christianity is a contemporary faith, although its roots go far into the past. It isn't enough to say about Christianity: "It was good for Paul and Silas and it's good enough for me." It must become my own, not because it suited them, but because it meets the deepest needs of my existence. The need for hope, joy, meaning and the need to love and to be loved—these haven't changed, but certainly the conditions of life have. People are really not asking for arguments that our faith is true; they want evidence of purpose and joy in our lives. Nietzsche's observation is pertinent: "Don't tell me about your Redeemer, let me see some redeemed people."

Everything on a bridge moves. Mobility and change characterize our age more than anything else. The person who doesn't like change is doomed to be unhappy in the twentieth century. The church can no longer be a stately cathedral calling men to withdraw from work and play in order to worship. Rather it must be a bridge which helps support them in their busy, dashing lives. It must also seek to link everything they do with the Creator of everything there is.

A bridge connects two areas that would otherwise be separated. The generation gap, the racial gap, the communication gap, the economic gap and the gap between the sacred and the secular all need bridging. If this book can help toward the bridging of some of these gaps, it will have fulfilled its purpose.

The book could never have been written without the inspiration and illustrations provided by family, friends and parishioners. These pieces have all been drawn from real life. The names, and sometimes the circumstances, have been changed in order not to embarrass anyone.

I have been indebted through the years to Professors Paul L. Holmer and Joseph A. Sittler, stimulating teachers and good friends. I am grateful to Dr. Robert McAfee Brown for reading the manuscript and offering helpful suggestions. My secretary, Mrs. Roland Power, somehow managed to look and sound Christian while deciphering things I wrote but couldn't read. My debt to William Robert Miller is unlimited. His editorial and theological radar prevented a number of literary disasters. Wreckage that remains belongs to the author.

Robert M. Herhold

Palo Alto, California

CONTENTS

Sacred Swingers

FUNNY, YOU DON'T LOOK CHRISTIAN

Have you ever watched people driving to church together?

Father and Mother are laughing at the kids, who are tussling and singing joyously in the back seat.

Suddenly the church building looms up.

"Okay, knock it off," Father commands.

A hush descends. Clothes are straightened and Bibles gathered up. A carful of somber faces arrives in the parking lot. They reverently close the car doors, and quietly march with Sunday faces toward the church. It is a look not unlike the one the parents had at P.T.A. while listening to their son play a trombone solo after only six lessons.

Some of us try to look Christian with lapel crosses, reversed collars and JESUS SAVES bumper stickers. Or we affect a strange tremor in our voice when we talk about religion.

People who fall over themselves being charming are deadly bores. When we try to look and sound Christian we blow the whole bit.

DISCIPLE IN A $50,000 HOUSE

Shirley lives in a five-bedroom home in an exclusive suburb. When a black family purchased a home in the community, Shirley invited the neighbors to her house to meet the new family.

She works with the Committee of Responsibility, an organization of doctors who bring wounded Vietnamese children to this country for treatment, and she has taken two children into her home until the war is over.

Shirley gives herself to bringing Christians together. With great feminine charm, she has conned ministers and priests into cooperating on a variety of projects, including worship services. Her living room was the scene of the first ecumenical dialogue in town. Out of this has grown a tutoring and assistance program to help inner-city children stay in school.

Not all of her efforts have met with success. She received anonymous threats and 3:00 A.M. phone calls after inviting the neighbors in to meet the black family. Her husband, Joe, was passed up for a promotion and eventually changed jobs because of her political activities. Neither of them regretted it, although they had anxious moments before he got another job.

When someone talks about the cost of discipleship, Shirley looks puzzled. She feels that she hasn't sacrificed much, certainly not materially. But she believes that the more you have, the more is expected of you. She can't bask in comfort while so much of the world is in misery.

Could the cost of discipleship mean living in a $50,000 house but being prepared to leave it anytime it gets in the way of being a Christian?

CINEMA VERITÉ

Once I saw a man taking a movie of his son throwing stones into a creek. The father directed every move the boy made. He told him when to pick up a stone, how to throw it, and when to wave at the camera. The boy was frightened and self-conscious, and his actions were stilted and mechanical. If the father had let his son enjoy himself, the movie could have been delightful.

4

God is not a super movie director. He doesn't give us cues for each situation. In Jesus, he shows us what it means to be truly human. From there on we have to play it by ear.

The nimble eyes that windowed a soul too large for pettiness and too sensitive for banalities, the look that said he was listening carefully, the probing, unmasking question—this and much more was Ed Nix.

He called himself an atheist or an agnostic because, inadequate as these terms are, they are better than the assembly-line religious labels people put on themselves. Ed found it difficult to say "Lord, Lord," but words like "peace," "care," "friend," were often on his lips.

What kind of a god didn't Ed believe in? The god of Sunday piety and Monday acquisitiveness. The antiseptic god of white altar linens for white parishioners only. The god who anesthetizes, systematizes, ostracizes. The god of we versus they, of believer versus infidel, of saved versus unsaved. Ed couldn't believe in such a god; he helped us to disbelieve in him also.

If you believed in the God of justice, Ed expected you to be just; if you believed in the God of love, Ed expected you to care. He took our faith more seriously than we did. He made us wonder if the real atheists weren't us, the ministers and pillars of the church. In his gentle way he was asking us to put up or shut up.

Ed never equated church membership with genuine faith. The church or synagogue you attended only told Ed where you spent a few hours a week. He wanted to know how you thought and lived the rest of the week. Ed knew that if God existed, he was too big to be worshiped only on Sunday.

Ed practiced what many preach. His was a religion of

6

empathy, a religion of rejoicing with those who laughed and suffering with those who wept. His religion opened doors, lifted barriers, demolished walls between men. He was a man for all seasons, a man for all colors, a man for all creeds.

CABLE CAR SANCTUS BELL

A group gathered in a downtown San Francisco plaza to break bread, to drink wine and to pray for peace. Apartment dwellers, out walking their dogs, paused to watch. The noise of the traffic composed the Gregorian Chant, and the clanging of the cable car pealed the Sanctus bell.

Instead of thin, tasteless wafers, they ate hearty sourdough bread. Some bearded and beaded youths strummed guitars to accompany the hymn singing. While waiting to receive the bread and wine, the worshipers talked quietly. Afterward, they continued their conversation at an English-style pub.

A church is where the Spirit and people commune together.

MARGARET

After a childhood accident, Margaret was paralyzed from the neck down. The excellent care of her parents and brother, plus her own courage, kept her alive.

Any time of day, people would stop at her home in Pittsburgh for a brief chat. She never gave them time to feel sorry for her as she bombarded them with questions about their activities and what was happening in the community. The postman, the milkman, the door-to-door salesman, the policeman, and clergymen of several denominations were all her friends. People left inspired by her faith and courage.

Whenever someone new appeared, Margaret asked him to sign her guest book. She had hundreds of names in it. When Margaret's friends traveled, they often sent her a postcard or a memento. The cards were put on display, along with several shelves of souvenir salt and pepper shakers, dolls and assorted bric-a-brac.

One day a faith healer set up a large tent on Pittsburgh's north side. Some well-intentioned people arranged to take Margaret there in an ambulance. They surprised her with the news.

Margaret was pleased by their gesture. But she said, quietly and firmly, "I'm not going. If God wants to heal me, he can heal me right in this room. I don't have to go to listen to any whooping and hollering to be healed."

Her friends were speechless as they struggled to comprehend Margaret's reaction. One of them finally said, "I guess you have more faith than we do, Margaret."

A PHILOSOPHER'S NEED

A friend who taught in the philosophy department at the University of Minnesota was confronted one day by a sophomore who had undertaken the task of educating the faculty. He had heard that the professor openly admitted to being a Christian. This the student couldn't believe. To the student, faith and intelligence were direct opposites.

The sophomore walked into the teacher's office, critically surveyed him from head to toe and said, "Say, I hear you're religious. How come?"

He expected the professor to recite St. Thomas' five classical arguments for the existence of God, and he was prepared to challenge each of them.

Instead the professor simply said, "I've got a need."

The need to overcome hopelessness and meaninglessness

will open a man to God sooner than will an argument for God's existence.

THE TEACHER

Martha teaches English in a slum high school. Many of her pupils come from homes in which there isn't even a newspaper to read. She knows that often they can't find a quiet corner at home to study. Some of them speak English only at school.

A few have imbibed the heady wine of racism and reject Martha because of her color. She understands why they feel the way they do, but it still hurts to be rejected. She tries to keep order so that some can learn, but most members of her class have known only chaos. She comes back each day to what sometimes feels like a beating.

After cooking dinner for her family, Martha often works late preparing imaginative lessons to interest her pupils. They are very proud of the newspaper they publish every week.

Martha seldom goes to church. For one thing, the sermons never seem to speak to the problems she has. She has big doubts about the God of 11 o'clock. But she knows that she needs more than her own strength to carry on. She prays a lot, even without using God's name.

NO NEED TO PLAY GOD

A World War II shrapnel wound in the back left Gary permanently confined to a wheelchair. He tried to work in an insurance office, but he tired very easily. At thirty, he resigned himself to living on a government pension as a 100 percent disabled veteran.

He taught in the Sunday church school, where his quiet courage was more important than any lesson taught from a book. Children loved Gary. Adults in the church considered him one of the most authentic Christians they had met.

Some friends invited Gary to attend a home Bible study group. He soon became an avid member and spent hours reading his Bible and filling out workbooks.

Soon he began to feel that anyone who did not share his religious experience or did not use the same language was not a Christian. He changed churches, believing that those in his former church were not "saved."

A friend wryly remarked: "Gary was a great Christian until he got saved. Now he plays God by trying to make us believe exactly as he does."

The trouble with playing God is that we humans aren't cut out for the role. Besides that, it messes up our real-life calling, which is to be truly human.

PLAYING AROUND WITH THE MENU

The man walks into the restaurant, sits down and accepts a menu from the waitress. After he has examined it carefully, she returns.

"May I take your order, sir?"

"I like the cover design of your menu," he says, "but I feel the format could be improved." He proceeds to make a number of suggestions on how the food lists and prices could be more artistically arranged and notes some typographical errors in spelling of items.

The waitress tries to hide her impatience, but finally she says, "But, sir, what are you going to order for dinner?"

The customer gives her a puzzled look and explains, "Oh, I'm not really interested in eating. I'm a connoisseur of menus."

Some people are interested in religion as a subject matter and will gladly discuss it over Scotch and water anytime. They may have a rare collection of Bibles and first editions on the religions of the world. They may also have majored in religion in college and kept up with the latest developments in theology.

But as far as Christianity is concerned, they are still playing around with the menu.

THE SQUARE

Cecilia doesn't understand why people march or demonstrate. Sometimes she thinks that the Communists are really behind it all. Hippies, draft card burnings, live-ins and activist clergymen all turn her off.

She has lived alone since her husband died several years ago. She doesn't complain or interfere with her children or grandchildren. When she feels sorry for herself, she suffers alone.

Cecilia doesn't understand why people in the slums can't get out by hard work and saving their money. Her family never had to ask the government for help. She cannot comprehend the disadvantages of being black or poor. How can she know what slum life does to people? She's generous to her children and grandchildren and is a reasonably soft touch for someone in need.

She goes to church to gain strength to carry on and to find help to be a better person. She doesn't understand why there is so much restlessness in the church, why ministers should get embroiled in controversial issues. She's deeply puzzled why the faith she grew up with isn't good enough for young people today.

Cecilia is a square. Cecilia just doesn't dig what's happening at all. But in the Lord's vast kingdom of swinging saints, isn't there room for some squares?

The Best Christian Was a Jew

LOX AND BAGELS ON A SUNDAY MORNING

It was summer vacation. We set up our tent in the Dunes State Park and then drove into Chicago to visit old friends. When our friends insisted we stay with them, we drove back to the park together to get the tent.

We had planned to attend church on Sunday morning. Then we discovered the delicious brunch prepared for us. As good as the food was, the conversation about religion and politics was even better. A Jew, a Catholic and two Lutherans, we found that the deeper the conversation ran, the more we had in common. As we passed the lox and bagels among us, the meal had a quality of the Holy Communion to it.

That Sunday the religious thing to do was eat lox and bagels with old friends.

A JEWISH BOSS

Catholic, Jewish and Protestant clergymen lobbied together for a civil rights bill in Washington in 1964. It was a rainy afternoon after one of the sessions. Ministers stood in huddled groups under a canopy at a side entrance to the Capitol, waiting for taxis.

As two rabbis got into a cab, one of them called good-naturedly to two men with backward collars: "Would you Gentiles like to integrate this cab with us Jews?"

"Thanks very much," smiled one of the ministers as he climbed into the cab. "Our boss is Jewish, you know."

THE BARGAIN-HUNTER

"Hey, Charlie, I just jewed down the owner two thousand dollars from his asking price on that house we wanted."

"What do you mean?"

"Well, I offered him four thousand less, but we finally split the difference. Believe me, he was a tough bird to jew down."

"Why do you keep saying, 'jew down'?"

"That's just an expression, Charlie."

"Are you Jewish?"

"No, I'm Lutheran."

"Then why didn't you lutheran him down?"

FUNNY, JESUS, YOU DON'T LOOK JEWISH

An artist once painted a nativity scene for the side of a church. He lettered above it: HE BECAME ONE OF US.

We may like to think of Jesus as being like us, a guy who would fit right in with the gang at Rotary. It comes as a shock to realize that Jesus was not a Christian, but a Jew.

How tempting it is to remake Jesus, rather than let him remake us.

TOO LATE, THE POISON

Marvin and Bill were not serious troublemakers, but they enjoyed whispering to each other in social studies class.

The teacher kept both boys after class and lectured them on their behavior. They solemnly promised to stop their kibitzing.

As they left, she called Bill back and closed the door. "You know, don't you," she said, "that Marvin is Jewish? If you two continue to be so close, the other boys will have nothing to do with you."

The warning came too late. Marvin and Bill were already friends. Besides, bigotry must be taught before fourteen.

Staid Churches and Subversive Christians

THE SIN AGAINST THE HOLY SPIRIT

People have worried about committing this sin and not knowing it. Theologians have tripped over themselves trying to define it. But the sin against the Holy Spirit is nothing mysterious: it is dullness. Plain, gray, risk-free, damnable dullness.

The theme song of some congregations is "A Mighty Fortress Is Our Church," and they defy the poor and the black, the hippies and the agnostics, to get in. The people inside are so busy polishing the furniture and running errands for each other that they pay little attention to what happens in the community. It wouldn't matter whether oxcarts or Mustangs went by the door. The sermons could be preached in the seventeenth century, and were.

Sometimes a church will erect an exciting building only to house the same old circle meetings ingesting missionary topics with peach cobbler, board sessions spending half the time on finances, Sunday school lessons answering questions no one asks. An elder or a deacon may be a gutty businessman, willing to take the big risk when necessary. But when he goes to church he assumes his most cautious outlook.

Instead of selling faith as a balm for tired businessmen or a celestial insurance policy, we could demonstrate it by the risks we are willing to take. If ministers were open to questions and rebuttals after a sermon (some regular members will panic), if the church would invest funds in ghetto businesses, if we would open dialogues with the New Left and the Far Right, if we would worship God as alive instead of holding wakes on Sundays, we could be rescued.

Jesus compared the Holy Spirit to wind. The sin against the Holy Spirit must be a vacuum in which nothing moves. When asked what he hoped to accomplish during his papacy, John XXIII flung open a window and said, "To let a little fresh air into the church."

PUTTING THE BITE ON SAINT PAUL

Five times I have received at the hands of the Jews the forty lashes less one. Three times I have been beaten with rods; once I was stoned. Three times I have been shipwrecked; a night and a day I have been adrift at sea; on frequent journeys, in danger from rivers, danger from robbers, danger from my own people, danger from Gentiles, danger in the city, danger in the wilderness, danger at sea, danger from false brethren; in toil and hardship, through many a sleepless night, in hunger and thirst, often without food, in cold and exposure.

From Paul's Second Letter to Corinth

Dear Paul:

Thanks for the latest account of your missionary adventures. Everyone has been asking about you. We look forward to your return and will have you down to speak at the Apollonian Club as soon as you arrive.

Paul, I am not quite sure how to broach this matter, but the straightforward approach is usually best. At the beginning of the year you pledged a gold shekel a week to the building fund. You kept your commitment for the first month, but since February we haven't received one shekel from you.

Now I'm sure that you haven't had the time you would like to devote to your tent business, what with getting shipwrecked and all. None of us wishes to interfere or to suggest to you how to run your business, but aren't you being a

slight bit impractical? After all, such activities as you describe are rather unusual for a stable businessman.

We hope to hear from you at your earliest convenience. We enjoy your letters and pass them around to the membership. Please understand my reason for mentioning the pledge. If we ever expect to build, we should do it before another wage hike drives construction costs sky high.

Faithfully,

Crispus

Building Fund Chairman
Church of Corinth

THE RELIGION OF FUND RAISING

The Bible for professional church fund raisers is a carefully detailed manual for reaching a financial heaven. Any ambitious leader, Christian or atheist, who follows each step can reach this goal.

The secret is to involve members of the church in doing everything from licking envelopes to estimating what others in the congregation can give. The most deadly sin is non-involvement. The man who spends a quiet evening at home with his family is vulnerable to the wiles of the devil.

One fund-raising firm instructs callers to pray three prayers. (Printed prayers are furnished if needed.) A prayer is said before getting out of the car, another just before the member fills out his pledge card, and a final clincher before the caller leaves. The member doesn't only have to worry about appearing cheap before a fellow member; he also has the Almighty frowning over his shoulder.

In some churches, fund raising has become a religion. Did Jesus die in order to raise the budget?

THE UNPROFITABLENESS OF BEING A PROPHET

Two soldiers in a cartoon look up at Jesus on the cross. One says: "Doesn't he know that he is only hurting his own cause?"

Every prophet from Moses to Martin Luther King Jr. has been similarly accused by people who don't understand their own and society's evil. The cross that decorates churches or is worn as jewelry is really a symbol of the willingness to kill a prophet rather than accept his pleas.

The prophet reveals the limits of society's tolerance. Martin Luther King Sr. said after his son's death: "They didn't kill Jesus for eating with sinners; they just criticized him for it. They didn't kill him for being a country preacher talking about love. They killed him when he went into the temple and began fooling with the power structure."

The cross is not a judgment on Jesus' sense, but on man's sin. The real tragedy is that we learn so little from the prophets' deaths when we could learn so much.

A BLANKET OR A SPORT COAT?

Peanuts fans are familiar with Linus' blanket. He drags it around with him everywhere as his source of security. The blanket is to Linus what cigarettes, liquor or other habits are to adults—as he points out to his critical grandmother, who drinks 32 cups of coffee a day. Linus goes into a severe depression every time his dirty old blanket is thrown into the washing machine.

In one strip, Charlie Brown asks Linus what he is going to do when he is too old to drag his blanket around anymore. He studies the problem for a moment and then replies, "I've been thinking seriously of having it made over into a sport coat."

Many people hold onto the church the way Linus holds onto his blanket. Like Linus' trauma when the blanket is washed, they get upset when anything in the church is changed.

People who want a religion safely garbed in the past usually prefer to hide from the tough issues of life. Lucy, in her know-it-all manner, tells Linus as he stands sucking his thumb and clutching his blanket, "You can't depend on that blanket forever, Linus. Sooner or later you'll find that out." Linus looks startled, and the next picture shows him with the blanket over his head and extending down to his feet. Lucy then says, "And you can't just withdraw from everything, either."

Instead of a blanket to clutch or to hide under, Christianity is a sport coat to be worn daily.

JESUS UNSAVES

"Brother, are you saved?"

Most of us are at a loss for words if we're ever asked this question. One reaction is: "Saved from what?" It could be salvation from further thinking or inquiry. A neat formula about Jesus is not the same as faith in the living God.

When an architectural student is "saved" by Frank Lloyd Wright and becomes solely devoted to that style, he usually stunts his own creativity. If a writer tries to compose sentences exactly like Ernest Hemingway's, he will not discover his own true talent.

Actually, Jesus "unsaves" us from slavishly imitating anyone, including himself. Jesus calls men to be his disciples, not his robots. Being a Christian doesn't mean dressing like Jesus, or being single and a carpenter. It involves being ourselves and caring and sacrificing in our own situation as Jesus did in his.

This relationship to Jesus is quite different from freezing him into a formula.

A BOUT IN THE NARTHEX

My first experience with a church fight came at the impressionable age of ten.

I was selected to be a Wise Man in the Christmas pageant, much to the amusement of my family. However, my mother let me wear her gold and red tablecloth in launching my acting career.

The other two Wise Men and I stood shivering in the cold narthex of the church, waiting for our cue to go down the aisle. As my tinfoil frankincense shook in my trembling fingers, I envied them. Their bathrobes looked warmer than my mother's tablecloth.

Suddenly, above the strains of "Silent Night," the voices of two ushers could be heard. They talked more loudly and gestured more wildly as they argued about which aisle we were to walk up. Finally, one of them socked the other. The other didn't turn his cheek. He punched back. We Wise Men stood by, growing wiser by the minute.

After this liturgical innovation, the two ushers expressed themselves to the pastor, who stood there like God on Judgment Day. One of the ushers finally offered to apologize if the other one would.

Most of us have a little more control over ourselves, but we frequently would like to sock an usher or someone else. Fortunately, the main thrust of Christianity is divine forgiveness.

THE WHOLE MAN

I once attended a church meeting in which a very hefty gentleman held forth on what he considered to be the chief weakness of the church today. Some people in the church, he said, were far too concerned with helping people in their physical needs, like housing and employment, rather than their spiritual needs. He said the soul, not the body, was the church's chief concern.

After at least an hour and a half of splitting the body from the soul, the rotund gentleman, who weighed more than 250 pounds, suddenly looked at his watch and exclaimed, "Why, we must all be famished. It's twelve thirty and we haven't had lunch." With that, he heaved his 250-pound soul up from the chair and went out to eat.

According to the gospel, you can't divide the soul from the body, especially at lunchtime. Christianity addresses itself to the whole man, body and soul. In one case, Jesus equated forgiving a man's sins with healing his paralysis. Both psychology and medicine affirm that many emotional and physical problems are related.

The church will lose the battle for men's souls if it turns away from their bodies. Birth control, racism, war and unemployment should be just as much a part of the church's concern as Holy Communion.

When Jesus left a memorial of himself, he did it with a meal.

THE HIPPIE

The young art student showed his admiration for Van Gogh by painting with the same swirling style and by wearing a beard like that of his idol. He came faithfully to church

and sang in the choir, even after his parents were divorced and left the church and the community.

Each Sunday he would arrive wearing a sweater, a T-shirt, slacks and sandals. He was the youngest man in the choir. I discovered too late that his fellow musicians delighted in kidding him about his appearance.

Finally the joke became old. The young man told me he was leaving the church because he was a pacifist and was joining a peace group. I told him that his church and pastor would support him as a pacifist and that I hoped he would stay.

Both of us knew the real reason he left.

MODEL-A FAITH

One of my earliest recollections of religious instruction is being driven to confirmation classes in a Model-A Ford. A friend's father would pick us up after school and give us each an ice cream bar to eat on the way. Between bites, we would practice rattling off the books of the Bible or whatever the lesson was.

Such an educational technique fits the modern world like a Model-A on a Los Angeles freeway. No longer can religious educators take for granted that young people believe in God, or if they do, that they have any idea what this belief means. The religious question for them is not what God did in ancient times, or what the five attributes of God are, or even if there is a God. The question today is what does God mean in a person's life—what difference does believing in him really make?

Anybody who can speak to the question of the function of God in young people's lives will have an audience. He doesn't even need to soften them up with ice cream bars.

DRAFTING GOD

In World War I, German soldiers went into battle with GOTT MIT UNS on their belt buckles. Americans believed with equal fervor that God was on their side.

We are glibly capable of identifying Christianity with personal, political or national interests. As heads are bowed in locker rooms, God is subtly requested to clobber the opponent. Prayers at political conventions often make God an honorary delegate. "Under God" in the Pledge of Allegiance can easily come to mean that God has signed his power of attorney over to the U.S.A.

Martin Luther spoke of making God into a wax nose which could be twisted into any shape. It's easy to turn the old hymn around and sing: "I am the potter, thou art the clay . . ."

PLEASE DON'T SMOKE IN THE POOL

The church's young people worked hard to prepare for Youth Sunday. Three of them carefully prepared brief sermons on the problems of communication with God and with people. One youth said the liturgy. Others read the scripture and led prayers.

Each did his or her part with poise and conviction. Most of the congregation responded with warm appreciation.

A few diehards worried about a teen-ager saying the benediction, and someone else chided the pastor about allowing a youth inside the chancel rail.

Some "sacred" traditions make as much sense to young people today as a sign saying: PLEASE DO NOT SMOKE IN THE SWIMMING POOL.

SHAKING THE STEEPLE

"How can you distinguish between a myth and a historical event in the Bible?" the young man asked the minister.

Then he inquired if the church had activities for unmarried adults.

Finally he got around to the reason for the appointment. "I am a homosexual," he said. "Would the church accept me as a member? Could I sing in the choir or teach in the Sunday church school?"

Underneath these questions, he was asking the minister: *Do you accept me?* and even, perhaps, *Does Jesus accept me?*

The minister knew it was pious nonsense to tell the young man that Jesus accepted him even though the church didn't. Most likely, the average church member would treat a homosexual as though he were contagious. The church steeple would probably crash down if a known homosexual were allowed to teach a youth class, even though he never tried to seduce anyone.

The young man believed that Christianity was largely a matter of living a good, moral life and that he didn't qualify. The minister said that no one is qualified, and that's why Jesus' acceptance of us as we are is such good news.

The young man said he would like to become active in the church, and the minister silently prayed that the steeple was securely fastened.

THE RELIGION OF ANTI-COMMUNISM

Bill and Mary were faithful workers in the church. Bill served successively as treasurer and then as president of the congregation. Mary was secretary of the Guild and superintendent of the Sunday school. All three of their children were active in the church's youth groups. Whenever something needed to be done, you could count on Bill and Mary.

Then they began listening to an anti-Communist radio preacher, who kept saying that the National Council of Churches was infiltrated with Communists and followed a line set down by Moscow. At first they dismissed this as overzealous talk, but after a while they began to wonder. With so much smoke, there must be some fire.

A new minister came to the church. He showed a great interest in human rights. Bill and Mary began to squirm when he talked about poverty and racism and said that the money spent on the Vietnam War should be spent to help America's poor.

Some friends invited Bill and Mary to a meeting of "patriotic" citizens concerned about the "drift toward Communism" in America. Soon they became active members of the John Birch Society. They quit the church and now spend all their spare time attending meetings, writing letters and talking to friends about the "Communist takeover" of America. Anti-Communism has become a new religion for them, and the John Birch Society is their church.

The anti-Communists succeeded in making Bill and Mary do what the Communists could never have done—give up the church of Jesus Christ.

MILK BOTTLES AND A FRAGILE REPUTATION

The pastor stayed late at the hospital with a patient and her family. At about 1:00 A.M. an intern suggested that they go home and get some sleep.

As the clergyman was leaving the hospital he met a member of his congregation, a special-duty nurse who was leaving work. The pastor offered her a ride home. They pulled up to her apartment, across the street from a family who belonged to the pastor's congregation.

The minister walked the nurse to the door. He heard the rattle of milk bottles being put out as he walked back to his car, then the crash and tinkle of glass as one of them slipped and broke.

As he drove home, the pastor realized that a reputation can be as fragile as a milk bottle. All it would take was a phone call to someone the next day saying that the minister was seen taking an attractive young woman home in the wee hours of the morning.

The White Hang-up

WHITE POWER

Imagine playing Monopoly with slightly altered rules. You are not permitted to own any property except Baltic and Mediterranean and the Water Works. Your opponent owns the rest with hotels. The cost of houses on Baltic and Mediterranean is the same as Boardwalk and Park Place. If your opponent doesn't like the number you rolled on the dice, he can assign you a number or have you sent to jail.

Black, red, brown and yellow people have found that this is the way white power works. The Indians' land was stolen and genocide was committed against them; black people were brought here in chains against their will; brown people have been exploited as migrant farm workers; and yellow people were thrown into concentration camps during World War II, while their property and businesses were confiscated.

Today white power works more subtly. A real estate man can make thousands of dollars on a deal without investing a penny of his own. All he has to have is good credit, a knowledge of the market and growth patterns, the ability to move in circles where prospective investors are and contacts with the construction industry. Then he can build twelve duplexes; ten will be owned by his limited partners, and two will go to him for his trouble. This is a perfectly honest deal which supplies good housing at a fair rental. But just try to put it together if you're outside the white power structure.

Another name for black power is black capitalism. Many talk about minorities getting better jobs, but few talk about people having a stake in the system.

One California real estate man is developing a training program to show minority people how to become owners and managers of real estate. After they learn how, the problem of changing the policies of banks and other investors still remains.

The question is not, "Would you want your daughter to marry one?" but, "Would you lend him half a million dollars to build twelve duplexes?"

BIGOTRY AND THE CHURCH CALENDAR

Don and Grace have been active in the same church all their lives. They attended Sunday school together, and Don was president of the youth group while Grace was secretary. Their parents were good friends and were delighted when the young couple announced their engagement. An Easter-size crowd attended the church wedding.

When Don and Grace looked for a home, their first thought was to locate near the church. They never missed a Sunday except for illness or vacation. Two weeks after Mark was born, Grace was back singing in the choir. Don has held every office in the church from acolyte to president of the congregation.

Almost all their friends are members of the church. They know few people of another religion or race. They have never been in a social gathering with Negroes, Orientals or Mexican-Americans. Their church and minister have done little to help them appreciate other people and cultures. Their total devotion to their own church's problems has narrowed rather than broadened Don's and Grace's outlook. They still think of Jesus as a good Lutheran who liked to attend church meetings and drink coffee.

Despite their sincere Christian faith, Don and Grace are racists. Due to lack of contact, they believe all black people are lazy, all Jews are sharp businessmen, and all Catholics get drunk before going to Mass.

The church, by only using Don and Grace to keep the institution going, has failed them. It has made them strong church members but weak Christians.

ACTING OURSELVES INTO NEW WAYS OF THINKING

For years, black citizens had been demanding that the city hire some black policemen. Each time the question came up there were strong objections from the white community; and the city council, also being white, went along with their wishes. Finally, the council acted with rare political courage and hired some black men anyway. Since then, most white people in the town have prided themselves on their councilmen's wisdom.

"You can't legislate morality. A change of heart must come first," opponents of change argue. But usually it just doesn't work out that way. How can it? After all, experience is what changes the heart. We usually enter a new situation with mixed motives—and then work things out. Fears are often dispelled and attitudes changed in this process of working things out.

A minister who served in the community that hired the black policemen put it this way: "People don't think themselves into new ways of acting. Rather, they act themselves into new ways of thinking."

A PART-TIME NEGRO

Taking twenty-three kids sailing is a hectic job at best. But if they are black, other people can make things a lot more tense.

Only five or six youngsters could fit into the boat at a time. Those waiting had the irresistible urge of all children to explore other boats in the harbor. If a white kid crawls on someone's boat, he is annoying; if a black kid crawls on, he is looting.

Things went better than I anticipated. The kids enjoyed the sailing and followed instructions to stay away from the other boats. Only one man gave us a hard time when he saw black children about to set sail on a white man's ocean.

It took a while for my stomach to settle down after being a Negro for one afternoon. I'm surely glad that I don't have that job full time.

ALMOST HUMAN

At a meeting of church people concerned about the racial crisis, a white man spoke up.

"We have got to forget about color. I have a number of Negro friends and recently visited one of them. As we sat across the kitchen table, I completely forgot that he was a Negro. It was just as if he were a human being."

THE REMOVABLE COLLAR

"I know it's not quite the same thing, but sometimes I can understand what it's like to be black."

"How's that?"

"Well, I'm a clergyman, and I wear a collar so I don't have to explain myself at hospitals, jails and other places."

"So?"

"People often treat me in a funny way, like I didn't put my pants on one leg at a time or something."

"You mean they think you're not quite human?"

"Yes, I guess that's it. They're always surprised to find out I know a carburetor from a transmission or that I notice when a pretty girl passes by."

"You do have a tough time."

"Well, it's just that a collar or a black skin causes some people to treat you as a special category of humanity. So you

see, black people and clergymen do have something in common."

"Except that you can take off your collar whenever you want to."

A CHRISTIAN EDUCATION

The high school senior confidently spoke his mind: "Negroes are better basketball players because they have a natural ability. They never study, but the teachers always pass them. The coach keeps them on the team even though they smoke pot and shoot heroin. They tear up any house they live in; they're lazy, immoral and . . ."

Nothing in twelve years of Lutheran parochial education had apparently shaken this boy's prejudices. The school required classes in religion and daily chapel. But no teacher had ever assigned him *Black Like Me* to read, nor did he study the causes of racism.

Such a school has a beautiful opportunity of relating Jesus' view of humanity to problems like war and racism. Instead, it settles for abstract ideas in the religion classes and nineteenth-century hymns in the chapel.

BRAINWASHED

The black student and I sat in the car talking after a college forum on the racial crisis. The conversation covered white and black power and the possibilities of violence.

Suddenly, the student swung the conversation around to himself and his uncertain status in a predominantly white, church-related college. He wondered if the students could ever accept him as he was.

"They think they're saying something flattering when they tell me that they often forget I'm a Negro," he mused.

The student looked me straight in the eye and said, "You know, your angular nose and Caucasian features are all right with me. But are my wide nose and kinky hair acceptable to you?"

Of course I said they were. But I wondered if I haven't really been brainwashed to think that white is more acceptable than black. And the tragedy is that the black student has also been brainwashed to think the same way.

THE PUT-DOWN

He was being honored by a service club for his citizenship and athletic ability. As the school counselor presented the award to the black youth, he said, "Walter is not only a credit to his race, but he has never been in trouble with the law."

The young man accepted the award with grace, but his stomach churned. He felt put down by the gratuitous reference to race and the automatic assumption that most black people are in trouble with the law. Later the counselor, who was a decent person, said that he was completely unaware of putting the young man down.

Racism is so often an unconscious, reflex action. But how do we become aware of an unconscious reaction? The angry voices of black America have been trying to shock our reflexes into new patterns.

PATERNALISM

The white principal of an African missionary school retired after thirty years of service, and he and his wife moved into a senior citizens' home built by the church. Soon afterward, a retired Army chaplain and his wife also applied to live in the home. When the ex-principal heard that his prospective neighbors were black, he immediately called on the manager of the home.

"Of course, I have nothing against these people," he began. "I gave my life to teaching the natives in Africa. But their way of life is different from ours. This Negro couple wouldn't really be happy here. We are such a closely knit group that they would feel out of place. I don't think it is fair to these people. Besides, it would create problems for the other residents . . ."

The principal "loved" the natives in Africa, but he never accepted them as equals. His whole image of himself as a superior white man reaching down to needy, inferior people would be shattered if he had to associate with black people as equals.

WHY NEGROES TURN BLACK

Arthur graduated from Howard University and served for four years as one of the few Negro commissioned officers in the United States Navy. After his discharge, he landed a good job as an electronics engineer in California.

He was never active in civil rights demonstrations, believing that progress for Negroes must be made through education and the courts. Arthur contributed to the Urban League and the NAACP, not to SNCC or CORE.

When he moved into a white, upper-middle-class neighborhood, four families in the block moved out. No other white people have moved in since.

When Martin Luther King, Jr. was assassinated, Arthur was on a business trip in the East. He had rented a new car. He was stopped by the police, ordered out of the car and forced to throw himself spread-eagle over the hood. He kept trying to tell them who he was, that his motel key and identification papers were in his pocket. Finally, after abusive language and many questions, including where he had got the car, the police let him go.

Black militants say that they do not have to work to make middle-class Negroes more militant; white people are doing the job for them.

CLIMBING THE LADDER

"Why don't they do it like the rest of us have done? My grandfather came here from Europe without a cent in his pocket, and before he died, he had a thriving business and a nice home. He didn't get any government handout either —he did it all by the sweat of his brow."

Many white Americans feel this way. They can't understand why black people can't do just as they have done. They forget several important differences.

No other group was brought to America as slaves. The black man's culture, religion, family life and even his name were stripped from him. For two centuries slaves were not permitted to marry. After emancipation, the black man had a much more difficult time finding work than his wife did. In case he got work and tried to become a man, he was put down by the title "boy" or "John." They didn't call him "mister."

His color prevented his melting into the American pot. No matter how successful he became, he was still a black man, which, to most white people, meant inferior. In case he persisted in being a human being, ingenious legal and illegal forms of discrimination were devised. A white immigrant has more freedom the day he touches American soil than a black American who has lived here all his life.

Poverty becomes a way of life for people. It starves their spirits just as it undernourishes their bodies. A few years in a slum ghetto will demoralize any group of people. After desperately trying to break out, people either give up in despair and become apathetic or they become enraged and riot.

For some citizens, the American ladder of success has broken rungs.

LIBERAL BLINDNESS

"We have met the enemy and he is us."

POGO

He's the popular minister of one of the large influential churches in town. He is a liberal who has maintained the respect of conservatives. The church has had people of several races in its membership for more than twenty-five years. When black people moved into the community during World War II, his church was the first to open its doors to them. It has been a mainstay in the Council of Churches, particularly in social action.

A few years ago when it was charged that there were Communists in the National Council of Churches, the pastor and board of the church met the issue head-on. They were among the first in town to take a firm stand for open housing. But now there are other issues, such as Vietnam, law and order, student unrest and drugs. They swarm like bees around the pastor's head.

The pastor has found their stings painful. Now he talks about the evils of riots and student unrest. He ignores the evils in society which produce these effects. When he is occasionally challenged by a militant young person, he indignantly points to his own and the church's liberal record. He has grown increasingly concerned about the church's ability to pay off a large indebtedness on its building.

The minister and the congregation continue to live off their liberal image. The fact that they have an integrated membership blinds them to the deeper injustices which maintain ghettos and poverty. Negro members of the congregation are often the most critical of militant blacks.

The issue in the church today isn't between liberals and conservatives. It isn't between integrationists and segregationists. It is between those who would protect the institution and its budget at all costs and those who are willing to risk not only the Sunday offering but possible crucifixion.

Grace Is Everybody's Friend

ALIVE AND WELL

Charles Evers, brother of assassinated human rights leader Medgar Evers, was in Los Angeles for a speaking engagement. Medgar's widow, Myrlie, invited him to her home for a reception afterward. Many black and white friends awaited his arrival.

Myrlie Evers had become concerned because her oldest son was becoming bitter against white people. He had a good reason. His father, shot by a white man, had died on the steps in front of his eyes. Myrlie Evers wanted her brother-in-law to talk with her children so they would not grow up hating whites.

Evers kept the guests waiting for more than an hour as he sought to help his brother's children forgive the unforgivable.

Jesus Christ is alive and well. He is living in people like Charles Evers.

JESUS IS A SHOCK ABSORBER

Taking your children to a movie can be a means of self-disclosure. The cashier told us there were good seats inside. We couldn't find them. We asked the manager for our money back. The refund was anything but prompt and cheerful. Then we split up because my daughter wanted to see one picture and my son another.

When my daughter and I went to pick up my son, the theater was locked. We went home, hoping he had called his older brother to pick him up. No Ted. We called the theater. A man answered, saying that the film was still running and he would come down and unlock the door.

When he let us in, I told him how annoyed I was that I hadn't been able to get in earlier. My tone was very similar to that of the first manager who had made the refund. Maybe it was a case of a chain reaction; one person's rudeness triggers someone else's. In any event, I couldn't help feeling a little foolish as he silently let me inside.

On the way home I wondered just why I felt so foolish.

Then it dawned on me—that man by his silence had "turned the other cheek" to my grumbling. Jesus did that. He broke the chain reaction of people wounding one another; when he was abused, he didn't strike back.

Jesus was like a shock absorber. His epitaph could well read: THE HURT STOPS HERE.

SLIP RENT FORGIVEN

Our family got interested in sailing one summer and bought a used sailboat. Then fall came and we had to move. We decided to sell the boat. After unsuccessfully trying to get rid of it ourselves, we consigned it to the company from which we had purchased it.

The salesman seemed to lack some of the enthusiasm he had displayed for the boat when he first sold it to us. It stayed in the slip for six months with only one customer interested enough to try it out.

The slip rent mounted as the value of the boat apparently decreased. Finally the owner of the boat company offered to buy it back. We had visions of his offering to take our boat for the rental on the slip, leaving us with enough to pay the taxes. Instead, we ended up with a little less than we paid for the boat, plus a summer of sailing. He also gave us a receipt marked: *Balance of slip rent forgiven.*

Sounds like a great idea for a religion.

BROWNIE POINT RELIGION

Moral push-ups and winning Brownie points—that's religion for some people. They hang mottoes on their walls, attend lectures on self-improvement and read books on building a "strong Christian personality." Such people set unrealistic goals and then become critical of their inability to reach them. They are even more condemnatory of the foibles and weaknesses of others.

When trouble and failure come for these people, their religion doesn't help very much. Rather than giving them new courage and hope, such a religion can even drive them into deeper despair. They need God's acceptance and help, but how can they get it with so few Brownie points?

The religion of Jesus Christ is 180 degrees away from this. We don't earn God's favor with Brownie points. It's a gift.

DESCENDED INTO HELL

He hadn't walked a straight line or drawn a sober breath for many years. I would visit him in his single miserable room in East Harlem. The windows were so dirty the room looked as if dark shades were drawn. A forty-watt bulb hanging naked from a cord emitted a feeble light. The only furniture was a sagging metal bed and a battered bureau with the knobs missing. The bed sheets were a tangle of dirty old rags. When my friend sat on the edge of the mattress, his disheveled self seemed to merge with the bedclothing.

One day, as we talked, with empty wine bottles and broken glass scattered about our feet, he pointed to a yellow, faded picture of Christ hanging on the wall. "You probably won't believe this because I don't look like a Christian,"

he said, "but that picture has kept me from taking my life many times."

When I say the words of the Apostles' Creed, "He descended into hell," I don't think of a place in the middle of the earth. I think of a room in East Harlem.

THE CLASSIFICATION SWIM

The "classification swim" is one of the first events that occurs after a new group of boys arrives at summer camp. The participants are rated according to their swimming ability and placed in beginner, intermediate and advanced classes.

At almost every camp period, along comes one boy who cannot swim but refuses to be classified as a beginner. He insists he can swim in spite of his obvious floundering. Days later this boy may come to the instructor and sheepishly say, "I guess maybe I can't swim as well as I thought. Could you help me a little?"

Only after this admission can the instructor teach the boy something about swimming.

Some say that God is dead. Others say that he has to wait until we discover that we need him.

THE LIFE OF A SALESMAN

The week begins before dawn on Monday as he drives to his first appointment.

If he's lucky, he can get in another call before noon. Sometimes he takes the customer out for lunch, and that means rushing to make his 2:00 P.M. stop.

After driving more than two hundred miles before noon, he's ready to call it a day.

Another stop at 3:30 and a quick check with another

customer at 5:00. This leads to cocktails until 6:30 when the customer has to go home to dinner.

The long, lonely evening begins. There are orders to send in, reports to fill out. But the salesman can't stretch his paper work out to fill up the evening. If there's a theater in town, chances are he's already seen the picture. There's not much left but the summer reruns on television. The days are okay; it's the nights that are rough.

He may eat at the best restaurant in town, but beans at home with the family would taste better than a filet mignon in solitude. This life may be all right for someone who wants to get away from home or who likes to chase women; it's not for a happily married man. But how does a natural salesman with a high school diploma make as good a living elsewhere for his family? He'd like to get off the road, but there are three kids he hopes to put through college.

Even though they may not look it, some salesmen are just as much heroes of the faith as the biblical guys with beards and long robes. What about putting a picture of a salesman and his car in the stained glass window of a church?

PAIN SHOTS AND GOD

Recently I spent seven weeks in the hospital for a series of operations.

I wish I could report that during this time I had a unique experience of God's presence and help, but I can't. During the worst of it I wrote the following impressions of how I felt: *drifting; mercy of others; mouth full of cotton; groggy; can't pray—God help me; loss of personhood; childish level; indifferent—what the hell; legs have iron bands; liquid diet; pain shot—where do you want it?*

It bothered me that I couldn't pray. The nearest I came to it was to ask Jesus to pray for me. I thought God must be sanity, and I was grateful that I hadn't lost mine. Most of the time I felt too lousy to care whether I lived or died. Somehow, I retained the confidence that God was with me either way.

Perhaps illness is a good time to get one's theology straightened out. Most of us identify God with prayer and with unique experiences we like to call "spiritual." These things aren't the same as God, and my experience seemed to be that the Almighty can function perfectly well without them.

Part of our human hang-up is that we think God should work as quickly and as obviously as a pain shot. If he did he wouldn't be God, but only another drug on the market.

Dead Men Do Tell Tales

COOKING FOREVER

The sweet young creature sets out to impress her boy-friend. She invites him to dinner, announcing that she will cook it with her own hands.

He arrives to pungent fumes of burnt roast. The biscuits are like bricks, and the coffee is thinly disguised lye. The boyfriend gamely downs the meal, longing for an Alka-Seltzer.

Then the sweet young thing comes to him. She runs her hands through his hair, sits on his lap, puts her arms around his neck and purrs into his ear, "Darling, let me cook for you forever!"

When we are told on Easter or at a funeral that we will live forever, we don't get too excited. Perhaps we are sick of this life and are not particularly thrilled by the thought of eternal indigestion.

Before we'll ever get excited about everlasting joy, we need some joy here and now. Christianity is a joy that begins now. Once we've acquired a taste for it, maybe we'll want it to last forever.

THE THEME SONG

Henry stopped in to arrange for his wife's funeral. Anything in the service would be all right with him, he said. Just one thing: "I'm asking the organist to play our favorite song."

When I entered the mortuary, I had to stop to get my

bearings. "I'll Get By as Long as I Have You," the popular song of the forties, was being played on the Wurlitzer organ.

"That's the song he requested," the funeral director told me. "It was their favorite. I had to hunt all over town to get the sheet music for it. He's in there listening to it with her now. He keeps asking the organist to play it over and over again."

How will Henry get by now that he doesn't have her? Christianity claims that the love they shared is part of God's eternal love. If so, can it ever be lost?

REQUIEM FOR A CLERGYMAN

The Reverend Harold Leonard Bowman, former pastor of Chicago's First Presbyterian Church, was a no-nonsense man in a profession in which it is difficult to be compassionate without becoming sentimental. His hurried, deliberate walk left little doubt that he knew exactly where he was going. His preaching was like lean beef, the fat carefully pared away. His prayers were like telegrams sent by a frugal son to a father whom he loved very much. When his wife died, he carried on like a man who believed the Easter sermons he had preached. When he retired, he moved into an integrated apartment building near the Loop.

Bob Bowman died as he lived. On Easter Sunday morning he got up early and baked two chocolate cream pies. A less secure man might hesitate to establish a reputation as a superb cook. He loaded the pies in his car and drove to the home of his daughter and her family. Then, after going to hear an old friend preach at an early service, he went to the service at his daughter's church. There he sat down in a back pew, picked up a hymnal and died.

Only the day before, he had taken his grandchildren to a play at a children's theater. Someone remarked how fortunate it was that he didn't have his fatal heart attack while driving the children in the car. But Bob Bowman would have first pulled the car to the curb, shut off the ignition, put a nickel in the parking meter and then died.

He was cremated according to his wishes. His apartment was dismantled before the end of the week. Relatives took a few mementos; the rest of his things were given away. On Saturday afternoon a memorial service, full of joy and strength, was held at the church he loved and served. Bob Bowman's life, death and funeral fit into a pattern. What he believed about God, his own life and purpose on earth, and the meaning of death was apparent. The funeral was not a sobbing, sentimental farewell. It symbolized a simple, dignified transition from life on earth to whatever God has in mind.

INNERSPRING CASKETS

The young man, wearing a dark suit and a porcelain smile, opened the door of the mortuary. The architecture and furnishings looked like a movie set from *Gone with the Wind*.

"Right this way, please," he whispered as though fearful of waking the dead.

The bereaved walked along the deep-pile carpet until they came to a room with a desk and several chairs. After polite introductions, the young man settled into a careful ritual of securing information about the deceased and his family. He silently estimated the type of casket they would probably select. Then he showed them the display room with more than forty models to choose from. It was like buying a new car with a wide choice of models, colors and accessories.

In rural communities, an old man would make his own pine coffin and leave it in the woodshed in case he died during the winter. Today we bury our dead in watertight vaults and innerspring caskets.

The affluent way we bury people may be an effort to

make the separation of death less real and painful. Or maybe it really amounts to an abandonment of the Christian hope, with the restoration of the body replacing the resurrection of the dead.

THE COMPETITOR

The long line of cars snaked into the cemetery. Harry had some friends and many business associates. They had come to pay their final respects to an old friend and a tough competitor.

Harry never liked to lose a deal. It wasn't the money that concerned him so much as the thought of being one-upped. He would take a loss on one of his drive-in restaurants before he'd let a competitor down the street beat him out.

He played it the same way with death. "Get me another specialist!" he shouted as each diagnosis revealed the fatal illness. One of his competitors quipped, "When the Lord calls old Harry, he isn't going to go."

At the end, he tried to beat the worms—he left instructions to be buried in a ten-thousand-dollar copper casket and had himself vacuum sealed like coffee. So no one would forget him, Harry ordered a towering monument for his grave. It topped all the others in the cemetery.

As the boys at the country club bar said after the funeral: "Harry sure was a tough guy to beat."

THE GOSPEL ACCORDING TO A CHICAGO CABDRIVER

George's faith is part of his job—not just because driving a cab in Chicago traffic requires enormous faith, but because he listens to the people he carries.

One night he picked up a woman at a hospital. She broke into tears as the cab pulled away from the curb. George let her cry for some time.

Finally, at a red light, he turned to her and said: "It's none of my business, lady, but did something rough just happen back at that hospital?"

The woman wiped her eyes, fought to control herself and said, "Yes, my mother just died."

The cabbie drove a few more blocks before replying. "Are you a religious person? A Christian maybe?"

"Well, I go to church regularly."

"What about your mother?"

"That I am sure of, she was the best Christian I have ever known."

"Lady, then why are you crying as if everything was over?"

A GLIB SOLUTION

An Easter church bulletin cover featured the resurrection. The painting displayed a radiant Jesus in freshly laundered garments strolling out of the tomb as though he were leaving a YMCA locker room. The guards, their heads resting in their arms, were like extras sleeping on cue in a Cecil B. DeMille movie.

Men will go on debating the nature of Christ's resurrection until they face their own. But if we could explain the resurrection, it would no longer be the work of God.

When there is truth in the form of unfathomable mystery, it is not enough to concoct a glib solution with a sentimental picture. If we settle for the picture, we miss the whole point of the resurrection.

Bridging the Gaps

THE YEARNING GAP

A Yale undergraduate gives his opinion of the generation gap: "When you have guys like William Sloane Coffin and Malcolm Boyd around, it's hard to talk about the generation gap in conventional terms. They're more radical than most of the students."

The gap is measured not in years but in yearning. Some high school and college students are as conventional as Calvin Coolidge. Some angry, middle-aged reformers have been trying for years to wake up the Establishment. The big difference is between those who accept, even welcome, change as the law of life and those, in the words of Adlai Stevenson, "who have to be dragged kicking and screaming into the Twentieth century."

The actions of hot-blooded youth who long ago dropped out of Sunday school will not change the church. Most of the young people who remain are fairly tame. The church radicals today are forty- and fifty-year-olds who have long been fed up with the church's maiden-aunt ways. They have decided to stay in the church and raise hell for heaven's sake.

But this is not unusual. Jesus, Socrates, Lincoln, the Kennedys and Martin Luther King, Jr. were all over thirty when they were killed for challenging the wind to change its course.

THE SHAVING GAP

A judge with gray hair was a delegate to a church convention. He rose to speak against a resolution recognizing the right of selective objection to war. Even though the resolution explicitly stated that someone who was conscientiously opposed to a certain war would have to suffer the penalty of the law, the judge claimed that the resolution undermined the rule of law.

A college student with a beard stood up. He spoke for the resolution. He said that the ancient Christian idea of a "just war" presupposed an "unjust war"; thus there is a duty to choose between them.

A television camera crew recorded the statements of the judge and the student, as well as a dozen or more speakers on both sides. That evening the local station showed only the judge and the student. They featured the best part of the judge's speech and the weakest argument by the student.

Appearances and position are all-important to those who lack true perception. The argument between a gray-haired judge and a bearded student is settled for many people without listening to a word either of them says.

Say, pastor, who's that hippie-looking character you have in your stained-glass window behind the altar?

THE CHURCH GAP

The pastor was being interviewed by the pulpit committee for a possible call to a large, affluent congregation.

After discussing all of the usual questions about pastoral work, Christian education and the organizations of the church, the prospective pastor asked the committee what they thought about social action. There was an embarrassing silence.

Then one sweet old lady with a flowered hat blurted out, "Oh, pastor, I'm so glad you brought this matter up. The social life in this congregation has fallen apart. Why, we haven't even had a potluck supper since our last pastor left us."

Another church, this one in a changing community, discussed the matter of ministering to black people. There was the usual foot-dragging and double-talk.

Then a young layman cut in: "This isn't primarily a question of whether we want black members or not. We don't even know if they want to join. The question is: Are we a church or a club? If we are a club, we're free to make up our own qualifications for membership. If we're a church, then this has already been decided for us by the New Testament."

Pardon me. There is a gap showing between your club and Jesus' church.

THE CONVERSATION GAP

Two men are carrying on an animated conversation in a jet airliner about the weather, politics and baseball when one turns to the other and says, "By the way, I'm Joe Smith. I'm a stockbroker; what do you do?"

"I'm Bill Jones. I'm a minister."

There is an immediate switch in the conversation. Joe's voice changes a little as he tells about his nephew who is studying for the ministry and what a fine thing this is. Then Joe explains why he doesn't attend church very often, but that churches are certainly needed today with juvenile delinquency on the rise, and so forth.

Bill nods politely and wishes they might return to the conversation of five minutes ago. He wonders if everyone feels obligated to talk only stocks and bonds with Joe. It isn't that Bill minds talking about his work or his faith. Quite the contrary. But he wishes Joe would accept him as a man and a pastor, not a spiritual truant officer.

Similarly, many white people, particularly liberals, feel that the only subject black people want to talk about is race. Liberals would be highly offended if someone told them that this is a form of racism. It's true that some black people are quite articulate about race, but this may be because that's the only thing most white people ask them about.

And then there is the white liberal on a jet airliner who discovers he's talking to a black clergyman. . . .

THE CONSULTATION

My fifteen-year-old daughter is an expert on parents, the generation gap and related problems. (May she still have this expertise after she has her own kids.) I asked for a little of her wisdom and was granted these nuggets of truth:

"In some homes all that the kids and parents have in common is the roof they live under. Some of my friends never talk with their parents about anything like sex or drugs or social issues because they're afraid there will be an explosion."

*   *   *

"Some parents either set a bad example like arguing with a traffic cop when the kid knows his parent goofed, or they set no example at all. They say: 'It's up to you,' or, 'You'll have to make up your own mind.' We like the freedom to decide things, but we also like to know where our parents stand. Either parents try to dictate to us or they don't seem to care enough what we do. I guess we want both freedom and guidance."

*   *   *

"Most of all, I think kids want to know that their parents back them no matter what happens. This doesn't mean that parents need to approve of anything you do, but it's good to know that if you smoked grass, your parents wouldn't disown you. Funny thing is that most kids who have this good a relationship with their parents don't have the need for grass."

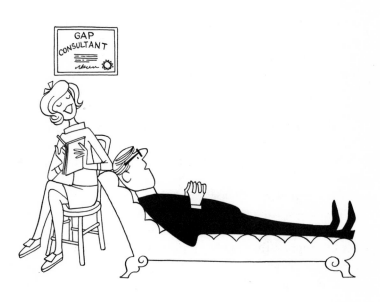

I thanked my daughter. "What is your consultation fee?" I asked.

Giggle. "You couldn't afford it."

DON'T BE SO UNDERSTANDING!

Steve and his parents were talking about his plans after high school. He felt the future was very uncertain, and that it was tangled up with racism and war. He questioned whether colleges really came to grips with these problems.

Steve's liberal mother and father listened thoughtfully to what their seventeen-year-old son said. They prided themselves on not being Establishment-type parents. After all his protests were over, they said reassuringly, "We understand how you feel."

His response was explosive and came from deep inside: "Stop saying you understand how I feel! How can you understand? You never had to face endless wars, drugs and all the rest of the problems we have. How can you casually say that you understand how I feel?"

The so-called generation gap—which may have more to do with sensitivity than age—is widened by the simple adult assumption that today's problems are, after all, just like yesterday's. Sometimes the truthful admission that we don't understand can lead to a more open-ended and helpful discussion.

Sex and the Single Couple

KEEP YOUR WIFE AS A MISTRESS

Paul and Barbara have been married for twenty years. They claim that marriage gets better all the time. They are not able to put their secret into a formula, but through trial and error and good fortune, they have discovered a few things that keep a marriage fresh and even exciting.

"You must work at making a good marriage," the manuals say. Paul and Barbara play at it. They have enough work to do in their careers. Paul is a minister, and Barbara became a teacher after the children were all in school. To them, marriage is not another vocation that demands strenuous striving. Rather, it has grown into an easy relationship characterized by play that is too important to become serious.

They can play together because they aren't interested in competing with each other. Having fallen in love with Paul rather than with the ministry, Barbara has never become a professional minister's wife. She supports him by being a good listener and occasional adviser, and doing a few things she likes to do in the church. Paul is interested in Barb's teaching, but helps her forget it at times.

After teaching school and being a minister all day, they enjoy being thoroughly comfortable and unguarded with each other. Sometimes soul talk, along with wine and music, is a part of their lovemaking. Occasionally, they manage to get away together on a short trip. Paul is delighted that Barbara has kept her schoolgirl figure and tells her so.

He feels he's made the best of two worlds—his wife and his mistress are the same person.

SURFING TO THE ALTAR

Guess Who's Coming to Dinner is a slick, successful Hollywood effort to deal entertainingly with the controversial subject of racial intermarriage. I left with mixed feelings when Spencer Tracy, after much agonizing reappraisal, finally agreed to his daughter's marrying Sidney Poitier.

Even though Sidney was a good catch, being Albert Schweitzer and Jonas Salk combined, I found myself resisting. The couple had known each other for all of ten days in Hawaii. The picture asked me to suspend all my disbelief and be enchanted with this brief courtship, simply because one party was black and the other white.

Suppose that instead of Sidney Poitier, the male lead had been played by Charlton Heston. Then what about ten days on Waikiki Beach as a sufficient basis for a marriage? Unfortunately, Spencer Tracy's legitimate questions were drowned out by the racial theme, and the romantic splashing of the surf in Waikiki.

PREMARITAL COUNSELING

This was no last-minute, shotgun affair. They came to see the minister a good three months before the wedding. They sat across the desk, cultured, self-assured, suburban, tanned from tennis. Their wedding had to be just right, not too lavish and not too modest. They had carefully picked out the church because it was the right size for the two hundred expected guests and they liked the sanctuary's warm, comfortable feeling. Would the minister advise about candles along the aisle, the bride's dressing room and the ring bearer and flower girl?

When the minister tried to turn the conversation to a consideration of what makes a marriage successful, he was greeted with polite silence. They finally mentioned words like "sensitiveness" and "compromise," but it was clear that they were more interested in discussing where in the service the soloist should sing.

They thanked the pastor for all his help. He said good-bye with the feeling that if God is invited to the wedding, he can sit with Grandpa and need not bring a present.

DISPOSABLE PEOPLE

The hand-lettered sign in the window reads: 24 HR. SPECIAL—2 EGGS, TOAST AND COFFEE—49¢. Two prostitutes enter and click by the young man with the dirty apron who is sweeping the floor.

It is very early in the morning, and the women look tired. They must be thirty—no, a closer observation indicates that they probably still drink illegally. They order black coffee with the 49¢ special and share a pack of Salems. One girl tugs at a false eyelash while the other kicks off her spike-heeled shoes. It has been a rugged night of walking, interspersed with "dates" at a cheap motel.

They sit in the all-night grill as dawn comes. They have been used and discarded like two disposable milk cartons. Why do they let themselves be used? Is it so lucrative? Do they think the fee they receive is a substitute for love?

No doubt a priest or minister once sprinkled water on their heads and prayed for God's grace. Who's to blame: Their parents? The church? Themselves? God? And what about the men who used them for a half hour and then discarded them?

THE GRADUATE

Early in the film *The Graduate,* an attractive, fortyish, married woman tries to seduce Benjamin, the young college graduate. As she suddenly appears naked before him, Benjamin exclaims: "Jesus Christ, Mrs. Robinson!"

At that particular moment the words "Jesus Christ" are no more than an expletive. As the film proceeds, Benjamin becomes more and more deeply enmeshed in a one-dimensional sex affair with Mrs. Robinson. The essential thinness of such an affair is pointed up by contrast with the growing love Benjamin experiences with her daughter. At the movie's end, he and Elaine Robinson ride off to an uncertain future. One thing seems clear, however. They care enough for each other that they are willing to defy conventions and struggle to find meaning for their lives.

Jesus Christ, Mrs. Robinson—that's what you're missing with your easy, superficial sex. Your daughter and Benjamin might not put it in these terms, but the spirit of Christ is where it's at. To put it another way, their love is bigger than sex—it involves freely giving of themselves to each other. It means being fully alive.

A GOD WHO LIKES SEX

It isn't quite proper for Christians to admit, at least in church, that they enjoy sex. Modern Puritans feel guilty about enjoying anything too much. Contemporary Victorians are particularly hung up about sex.

They have been taken in by a theology which suggests that although God is good, his creation of sex was at best shady. Certain people have therefore concluded that a celibate life is more pleasing to God than a married one. Others have married but have usually felt that God was too busy listening to the prayers of celibates to bless their lovemaking.

It is not enough to say that sex is not sinful. Sex is a remarkable gift from God. Instead of the old Puritan-Victorian hang-up about enjoying sex too much, two persons who have become one have the joy of complete freedom.

MAYBE EVERYONE SHOULD BE MARRIED TWICE

Most of what the church says about sex is negative. For example: "Thou shalt not commit adultery." Sex is considered bad except in the marriage bed. Then the church has the problem of how to create an instant good out of what has been a constant evil.

Does an hour's interview with a clergyman plus a fifteen-minute ceremony really make two people one and sex good? Is there any assurance, after all the candles are snuffed out and all the rice swept up, that a couple is mature? To say that a ceremony makes all the difference is to confuse Christianity with magic.

A few words mumbled at the altar while the couple hold sweaty palms doesn't make sex good or a marriage "Christian." The goodness of sex is discovered as two people become turned on to the deepest needs of each other. Sex is not just what a couple do when they climb into the sack. It is what they are to each other all the time, in and out of bed. This caring and sharing is what makes sex good, not the candles and rice, or even the words of the minister.

Maybe the church should have two marriage ceremonies: one to bless the physical union and another as a "confirmation service" when the couple begins to discover what marriage is all about.

HO-HUM SEX

Arnold, a successful, thirty-five-year-old businessman, is talking with a minister regarding what he described as a "ho-hum" sex life:

"Pastor, Katherine and I have really worked at trying to improve our sex life. At least I have. We've taken vacations together alone. I urge her to buy sexy clothes and I always compliment her on how good she looks."

"Does this help?"

"Not really. There just isn't any kick left in sex for us. It's the same old thing each time."

"You feel sexual intercourse is· *the* problem?"

"Well, isn't it? That's what all our dissension seems to be about."

"Do you think that your problem might be intercourse —period?"

"What do you mean?"

"Sexual intercourse is only one part of the whole problem of communication between husbands and wives."

"Maybe so, but I still think our main problem is sex."

"What would you say to a merchant who said his business is failing because he isn't taking in enough money?"

"I'd tell him to look into the reasons why he's losing money. It could be a whole combination of factors."

"Couldn't the same thing be true of sex?"

Piety and Politics

HUMOR AND POLITICS

John F. Kennedy once gave his old friend Dave Powers a cup inscribed: *Three things in life are real—God, man's folly and laughter. Since the first two are incomprehensible, we must do the best we can with the third.*

Humor makes men humane. It involves a recognition of the final absurdity of all our pretentions.

Humor is essential to a democracy because it enables leaders to distinguish between themselves and God. Dictators never have a sense of humor. Carl Sandburg wisely included Lincoln's laughter and his religion in the same chapter of his biography.

It is far better to be governed by a humorous man who never mentions God than by a humorless man who confidently thinks he speaks for God.

CATCHING UP WITH JESUS

Both the church and the city wanted a successful young businessman to serve on their councils. The church was going smoothly, and there were enough candidates for its council. The city, on the other hand, had gone through a recent scandal involving several councilmen.

The pastor urged the young businessman to run for the city council. "We need you, but not nearly as much as the city does," he said. "God's work is done at city hall just as much as it's done in church."

Maybe someday we Christians will catch up with Jesus, who spent most of his time with people in the world.

A PREVENTIVE GOOD SAMARITAN

An accident once a week at a busy intersection in front of the church was not unusual. Some of these accidents involved serious injuries. There were no stop signs, and the location of the church and two apartment buildings made it a blind corner.

Repeated letters, phone calls and visits to the police, traffic engineers and alderman were made. Only vague promises to "study the problem" resulted. One day, after a particularly bad accident, the pastor of the church called the traffic division of the police department and held the phone outside the window so the sound of the ambulance could be heard. Still no stop sign.

Finally, the pastor attended a political meeting called to generate enthusiasm for the alderman's reelection. He complained about the absence of the stop sign. In less than a week there was a sign on the corner.

A neighbor, upon learning of the political pressure necessary to get the stop sign, said to the pastor: "I've always had the image of the church as being interested only after people have been injured, and then calling an ambulance. I'm happy to see that you are the kind of Good Samaritans who try to *prevent* people from being clobbered."

KEEP FORGETTING

President Kennedy once held a door open for Mrs. Eleanor Roosevelt, but she gestured for him to go ahead.

"Remember, you're the President," she chided him.

"I keep forgetting," Kennedy replied.

Men like Hitler and Stalin would not have forgotten. Identifying themselves with the power of their office, they

became despots. Maybe there is something in the spirit of democracy that produces a different kind of greatness. Somehow we feel more comfortable when the man we entrust with power keeps forgetting.

THE BRIBE

"Could I see your driver's license, please?" The youthful driver took his license out of his wallet and handed it to the officer. "You know, you just made an illegal left turn," the policeman continued.

The youth's father got out of the car and stood next to his son and the officer. "But, officer, there wasn't even a sign prohibiting a turn here," the father said.

After considerable debate, the policeman lowered his voice and said, "If you don't want a ticket, that will be five dollars."

The youth's roommate got out of the back seat. He showed the officer a card indicating that his father was the chief of police in another community.

The officer smiled, returned the card and said to the driver, "Be more careful next time, son."

As they drove off, the father remarked how glad he was that they didn't corrupt the young policeman.

The son replied, "Don't be too pious, Dad. The cop is already corrupt. We were ready to give him the five until he let us go because of Ken's father. If we really cared we would be concerned about the kind of miserable salary a policeman has to live on."

The father, who considered himself a just man, painfully realized that his son understood more about justice than he did.

HALF A CRATE OF STRAWBERRIES

The roadside produce stand was just closing when we stopped. The owner offered to sell us half a crate of strawberries for a dollar because he couldn't keep them for another day.

"What a bargain!" we exclaimed—less than ten cents a box. We were so elated that we forgot it was a bad deal for the pickers and salesman.

Some men get killed in a war that makes other men rich.

Slum tenements yield a higher return on the investment dollar than does middle-class rental housing.

Maybe love means trying to organize life so that our good fortune doesn't depend upon another's misfortune. The strawberries had to be sold or they would spoil. But why must men continue to become wealthy over the victims of war or the misery of slum dwellers?

THE REVOLUTIONARY

Mike stood up at a meeting of radical white students who hated the Establishment and wanted to bring in a new world of peace and freedom. He said he would not fight in Vietnam or in any war.

The talk swung around to the black-white crisis, and Mike said he might find himself shooting white cops. An outsider suggested that he join the Marine Corps in order to learn to shoot straight. Another person asked if he would shoot black cops.

Mike's most serious problem was not that he condoned evil to bring about good, but that he didn't know why he was angry. Some whites may support a black revolution not because they love black people but because they reject themselves and other white people. Such people make shaky allies in any cause.

The business about loving your neighbor as you do yourself is the most revolutionary idea.

TIME TO THINK

The question to the eighth-grade confirmation class was: "What difference would it make in our society if people observed one day a week as the Lord's day?"

The answers ranged from cutting down the crime rate to ending wars. One girl sat quietly skeptical, so I asked her for her opinion.

"I don't think it would make the big difference that everyone says it would," she replied. "But maybe we would have more time to think before we did things."

The Loose Offering

THE WORLD BY THE TAILPIPE

They live in a large apartment building overlooking the ocean near Santa Monica. The management caters to the young unmarried jet set. They're well-educated, talented people who make their living in the entertainment, aircraft and electronics industries. They work hard from Monday through Friday so they can play hard on the weekends. A paycheck that represents long days of labor is worth blowing on one flight to Waikiki Beach for a big bash.

Late Friday afternoon they climb into their Jaguars and Thunderbirds. Sometimes several of them get in a racing boat and spend a weekend on Lake Mead. They seem to have the world by the tailpipe. They have everything *Playboy* says a young man needs for the abundant life: money, cars, boats, women, booze and a long weekend.

The jet set has something in common with authentic Christians: both work and sacrifice for their gods.

MUSICAL CHURCHES

Ralph is a perfectionist. As the foreman in a printing plant, he sometimes makes a man reset a job before the customer has seen it. Other times he will set the job himself rather than trust it to someone else.

His home life is much the same. He sniffs out the dust on the piano and criticizes his wife for giving the children a nickel over their allowance. Dining out with Ralph can be a nightmare; people hold their breath to see if he will send his steak back to the kitchen.

Religion for Ralph means keeping a set of rules. He sees God as the Supreme Bookkeeper, carefully noting all infractions on a giant log table. Ralph has added a few rules about drinking and dancing that the Almighty hadn't considered. Frequently the family hears two sermons on Sunday —one by the pastor and the other by Ralph on what was wrong with the sermon.

Ralph plays a game of musical churches. Every few years he changes his membership, thoroughly convinced that everyone at the last church was a phony.

Too bad Ralph has never understood Christianity. He would have discovered that it is not a religion of up-tight rules but a declaration of our freedom in God's acceptance of us. If he ever bought this idea, Ralph might be easier on himself and those around him.

DOES A CHRISTIAN KICK A DOG?

I thought of myself as a canophile. I would always defend a dog, be he underdog or not. When all of this changed, no one was more startled than I.

Two other families had given up on the six-month-old Yorkshire terrier when the veterinarian donated her to us. It seemed she had trouble distinguishing between the living room rug and the bushes outside. And she cried all night for reasons best known to a Yorkshire spinster.

Our family likes challenges, so we decided to provide a Christian home for her. She immediately mistook our rug for a bush. She cried all night.

One day when I was inviting her out of the house, she stopped halfway across the doorsill and refused to budge. I nudged her with my toe. This was my first act of brutality against a dog, and I suffered pangs of conscience. But remorse faded suddenly one morning when she crawled by me on her stomach after she had hysterically sobbed all night. That hang-dog expression after my loss of sleep drove me mad. I kicked her. It wasn't a toe nudge. I honest to God kicked her. My daughter's look told me just what kind of monster I had become.

I felt terrible. I went into my study and brooded. In the space of a few weeks I had changed from a kind young man to a mean and dirty old reprobate who kicks dogs. What would I do next? What kind of demon was being unleashed inside me?

My understanding daughter suggested the children stop bringing the dog inside the house when she cried earlier in the evening. Instead they might even go outside and whack her lightly with a newspaper. It sounded like the beginning of a rehabilitation program.

I was so grateful that I licked my child's hand.

IT'S ALL TAX DEDUCTIBLE

Mark is a partner in one of the fastest growing ad agencies in New York. He works hard and is hungry for success. Since much of his business is transacted over drinks and dinner, Mark is often away from his Connecticut home three or four evenings a week. He tries to include his wife, Lynn, when possible. But when she does go, she feels completely left out of the conversation.

When they attend parties together, Mark is the usual center of attraction, and he and Lynn often do not say a word to each other all evening. She often wishes she could run away, but where? There is one escape which is readily available: booze. After four or five martinis, Lynn doesn't care what anyone talks about. She also found out that a few drinks before Mark arrives home on the 6:15 eases the tension between them. She floats through dinner and usually falls asleep right afterward.

Everything Mark does is calculated toward advancing

his career. He doesn't just have friends—he has useful and influential friends. He doesn't entertain or go to parties for pure enjoyment—it's all part of his business; it's all tax deductible.

Judging from Mark's income tax bracket, he's a whopping success. But what does it profit a man if he gains status on Madison Avenue and loses his soul?

SIN MAY BE AN OLD CHEVROLET

I owned a 1931 Chevrolet when I drove between home and the University of Minnesota. It frequently broke down, making me late for class or causing me to miss classes altogether. A box of automobile tools soon became more essential to my education than my textbooks were.

One day some youngsters began laughing as I drove by. I barely heard one of them shout: "Hey, your wheel is coming off, mister." I was still smiling at their childish sense of humor when my car started listing to the right.

Half of the rear axle had worked loose from the differential, causing a wheel to protrude a foot or two from the side of the car. Since hiring a tow truck would have cost as much as the car was worth, I waited until a friend could push me home.

I didn't learn the meaning of this lesson until two or three old cars later. I had begun by thinking I needed a car to get to school, but it became apparent that the car needed me more than I needed the car. I finally had to choose between collecting ancient wrecks and getting a college education. When I started taking the bus to college, my grades improved.

Sin is anything that gets in the way of fulfilling God's purpose for a life.

It might even be a 1931 Chevrolet.

TRAVEL FOLDER THEOLOGY

At the beginning of each year I receive several travel folders describing group plans for ministers to visit the Holy Land. Somehow I have never been too attracted by them. It is partly the cost, but also that I suspect I would see scenery not too different from parts of California. Sometimes the writers of Holy Land travel folders get carried away and suggest that rich religious rewards will accrue to the tourist. No doubt one could return with a set of slides for a women's circle, but that is not exactly a great renewal of faith.

Being a Christian doesn't mean walking over the geographical area where Jesus walked. It means covering a different kind of ground—entering into situations of suffering and need where Jesus is.

THANKS

One Sunday afternoon my nine-year-old son and I went surfing. More accurately, I carried the board and hoped he wouldn't ask me to ride it. As we watched the whitecaps charge the shore, he saved face for both of us by announcing that the water was too rough for surfing.

Instead we dove madly into the leaping waves and let them smack us around. Like the Light Brigade, we hurled ourselves at the foaming foe. We shouted our defiance at each crashing breaker as, man and boy, we battled the sea.

Finally, with smarting eyes and tingling bodies, we started for home. My son turned and said, "Thanks for taking me, Dad."

Whom do I have to thank for crashing breakers and a nine-year-old son who likes to charge them? My lucky stars? The Great Pumpkin? God?

If there were no God, I'd invent one so there would be someone to thank.

A GRASS RACE IN A PIE TIN

Several years ago a group of people conducted a "scientific" experiment. They filled a large pie tin with rich soil and planted it with grass seed. Then they placed a divider in the center of the pie tin. Both sides had the same soil, the same seeds, the same amount of sunshine and moisture.

Then the group prayed for the seeds in one half of the tin. No intercession was offered for the other half.

Sure enough, the grass on the prayed side grew not only greener but taller. Surely this proves that prayer is answered, said the experimenters.

Some skeptics felt it raised more questions than it answered. Would God enter into a fun-and-games experiment with prayer? What kind of prayers were offered when the goal was a grass race in a pie tin? Someone quipped that the grass in one side grew faster because of the moisture from the breath of people praying.

Prayer, like faith, cannot be scientifically demonstrated.

God promises to answer our prayers, but how he does it is still up to him. Otherwise, he becomes a giant soft-drink machine and we can kick him when we get root beer instead of Coke.

LETTING OUR BOYS DOWN

The young man used to belong to the Boy Scout troop at our church. Then he grew up and went to Vietnam. I went to visit him at a nearby military hospital, where he was receiving treatment after a grenade exploded in his face, leaving him totally blind.

He hadn't accepted the fact that he would never see again. When I tapped him on the shoulder and explained who I was, he thought he was back in Vietnam and asked if I had brought him some ammo. I felt overwhelmed and became speechless. My nineteen-year-old son was the same age as many of the wounded G.I.'s in the room around me.

A young patient, paralyzed from the waist down, had a small American flag above his head. When asked how they were doing, he and other critically injured men gamely answered, "Much better, thanks." Another youth was the only survivor of a helicopter crash. Most of his body was covered with charred and seriously burned flesh. It was hard to tell just how these men felt about their misfortunes, since they all put up such a good front.

Critics of the Vietnam War are often told they are letting our boys down. I felt I was letting them down because I have done so little to make known my opposition to that senseless and immoral war.

THRILLED TO DEATH

Bonnie and Clyde are hiding out in a dreary tourist cabin. He offers her a chance to leave him and get away. "You know if you stick with me you'll never have a moment's peace," he tells her.

Her reply is a mixture of love and innocence: "Is that a promise?"

The boredom of a dusty Kansas town and the excitement of the chase are the movie's explanation for the career of Bonnie and Clyde. We identify with them because there is something in us that flees boredom and seeks excitement.

We have mixed feelings about Bonnie and Clyde. Their form of excitement was sick, of course, but why did many in the movie audience cheer when they shot their way out of a police trap? Were Bonnie and Clyde any sicker than nations who give their highest medals to people who practice violence?

There's something deep inside all of us that is fascinated by violence. But if we don't find some new forms of excitement, we'll be thrilled to death—all too literally—by the old ones.

SOLID GROUND

Paul Tillich's description of God as the Ground of Being used to leave me cold. It seemed too impersonal to have much meaning in my life.

Then I spent some time in a hospital. I felt pushed physically and psychologically as far as I could imagine going, but life held together. I had hit bottom and found that it was solid.

God did not speak to me, with or without drugs. He did not whisper in my ear "while the dew was still on the roses." The only voice I heard early in the morning was the matter-of-fact tone of the nurse telling me it was time to take a sitz bath.

The more I expect God to act in obvious ways, the more he eludes me. Sometimes illness or adversity gives us not a profile of God, but an experience of his strength and concern. I discovered a solidity at the depth of my existence which I can only call "God."

A MAN AND HIS CAR

The owner of the brand-new, sleek, shiny sedan was a junior executive with a large company. His wife didn't think they could afford a new car just then; when he brought it home they had a terrible fight. He spent more time washing and polishing it than he spent playing with his children.

After two years he traded it in on a newer, sleeker model. An Army sergeant bought the sedan and loaded his wife and three kids in it for a trip across the country. The family sang songs, played Password and enjoyed looking out the windows. They whizzed over the Great Plains, soared up the Rocky Mountains and glided across the Golden Gate Bridge.

Many miles later, the sergeant sold the sedan to a young man buying his first car. Again, it received the same tender, loving care as it had from its first owner. In fact, the third owner treated the car better than he did his girlfriend. When he made love to her on the worn back seat, it was more like rape.

One night the young man had a violent quarrel with his girl. He drove so fast that it was impossible to make all the turns on the road home. The car left the road, hurled across a ditch and hit a tree.

If you want to know what a man is really like, observe him with his car.

WHAT THE SNAKE SAID TO EVE

A theologian once lectured a group of seminary students on the creation story in Genesis.

When he was through, one student rose to ask: "Professor, are you trying to tell us to believe that a snake spoke to Eve?"

"It's not important to believe that a snake spoke to Eve," said the professor, "but it is quite important to listen to what he said."

Today the snake might slither up to Eve and say, "Hey, baby, you dig that fruit, don't you? God's no square, so grab yourself some and live it up."

The snake cons us by making evil appear as good. He offers us quick and easy ways to succeed in life. Perhaps he

suggests that we make a fast bundle of money so we can "do some good."

What the snake always implies is that there is a better life than the one God gave us.

THE HAIRCUT

"Just trim a little around the ears," I told the barber.

"Don't you want the sides and back thinned out?" he asked, almost with a hurt expression. "What about the top? That ought to be cut down some, don't you think?

Did he think he wasn't going to earn his fee? Was he afraid he was aiding and abetting a prospective hippie?

I agreed to let him cut a little more, since it seemed to mean so much to him and it was only my hair. But I cautioned him not to cut too much.

Halfway through the haircut, I looked up from my magazine to discover that my barber friend was scalping me. I shouted halt, and he reluctantly withdrew his shears. As I looked at the denuded sides of my head, I wondered what would have happened if I asked for a close trim. It would undoubtedly have required surgery.

Like the barber, most of us find it hard to resist improving upon other people. The belief that we know what is best for others has led to everything from short haircuts to wars.

A DRAWERFUL OF REJECTION SLIPS

Next to an understanding wife, a writer needs a good editor. Few authors are objective enough to know infallibly what should be rewritten and what discarded. An editor is a hard-nosed but strangely sympathetic surgeon who can give a hearty bill of health, dispassionately suggest needed surgery, or even recommend mercy killing.

A writer needs other writers with whom he can share his trials and frustrations. It helps to know that they too have a drawerful of rejection slips. Most of all, it helps to know that, despite the rejection slips, they believe they have something to say and this fact will someday be recognized.

A Christian needs other Christians. He needs someone who cares enough to tell him the hard truth, with love. He needs other Christians with whom he can share his triumphs and mistakes and sins and learn from them that God never issues a final rejection slip.

Another name for these other Christians is the church. The church is much more than potato salad and solemn assemblies; it is sharing common burdens and common joys.

Afterword

William Robert Miller

What kind of man writes a book like *Funny, You Don't Look Christian?* A former varsity miler? A Merchant Marine purser? A newspaperman? The moderator of an interfaith television show? If you guessed any one of these, you would be partly right, because Bob Herhold has been all of them. The other part, if you were meeting the author for the first time, might not be so obvious, for at forty-four he still looks more like a college athlete than do most Lutheran pastors, imagined or real.

Robert M. Herhold was destined for the ministry in no cut-and-dried conventional way. Both his grandfather and his father were Lutheran counterparts of the stern Puritan businessman known so well to American history and literature. Like others of his generation, Bob Herhold reacted against that background, yet found himself "bugged by God" and inescapably gravitating toward an outlook on life that was more Christian in content than in outward form—an outlook sensitive to human need and unfettered by excessive doctrine.

The externals of Herhold's childhood and youth are typically American—public schools, wartime service in the U.S. Army Air Corps, then undergraduate studies at the University of Minnesota, majoring in sociology and serving as a social caseworker for Big Brothers, Inc. It was at Minnesota that he was a member of the varsity track team. During summer vacations he worked as a merchant seaman and as a camp counselor. A member of Alpha Delta Phi, in his senior year he and classmate Don Fraser conducted a campaign to eliminate racial discrimination in fraternities. It was Herhold's introduction to the struggle for human rights in America. Like Fraser, he might have gone on to a political career—Fraser was later elected to Congress. But some inner impulse prompted him instead to enroll at Yale Divinity School. He received his Bachelor of Divinity degree from Northwestern Lutheran Theological Seminary in Minneapolis, and was ordained to the ministry in 1951. He married Muriel Louise Townsend, of whom he says, "More than anyone else, she has helped me to understand the style of a secular Christian." Twenty-one years of marriage and four children have, for Herhold, added up to a real experience of God's grace. Muriel Herhold has a mind of her own and a career of her own, as a teacher. Her husband is glad she has not in all these years tried to fit herself into the role of being a "minister's wife." If she ever does, says Herhold, "that will be the day I leave the ministry. I don't mind being a minister nearly as much as I would mind being married to a minister's wife."

Herhold's first two pastorates were to inner-city Lutheran churches—Bethel in Pittsburgh and Woodlawn Immanuel in Chicago. His sociology background did not go to waste, nor did he forget his commitment to racial justice. At Bethel, Negro children had been literally turned away from Sunday school. Herhold submitted his resignation, and enough people rallied behind him to enable him to stay on and implement an open-church policy. In Chicago he received the James M. Yard Brotherhood Award for similar efforts.

He has not only been involved in gestures of brotherhood but has more than once put his career in jeopardy for the sake of his convictions. Moreover, he is among the very few white churchmen who, in and out of season, has *listened* to the angry voice of black America and can "tell it like it is." It is no easy step for a minister to offer his resignation to make a point. Herhold does not consider himself a militant, but he advises young men entering the ministry to have an alternative occupation to fall back on, just in case. He thinks this is a sensible precaution not only in the racial context but because he believes, along with Harvey Cox and John A. T. Robinson, that "the ministry is going to undergo some sharp changes in the next decade or two."

Herhold's own ministerial career has been varied. After Woodlawn, he was pastor of suburban St. John's Lutheran Church in Mound, Minnesota. Here he and Muriel became active in the Minnesota Democratic Farmer-Labor Party, and in 1960 Bob went to Los Angeles as an alternate delegate to the Democratic National Convention. He was asked to run for the Minnesota Legislature, but didn't see how he could do this and still remain pastor of a good-sized church. Writing in *The Lutheran*, he asserted that God "is concerned with all that happens to us on earth—including our politics." The pastor's churchly office, he said, "doesn't strip him of his political or civic responsibilities," although he must make it clear that the minister in partisan politics is not speaking for the church—"Jesus did not organize either the Republican or the Democratic party."

In 1961, for family health reasons, the Herholds moved to Tucson, Arizona, where Bob set aside his clerical collar and took a job as a reporter for the Arizona *Daily Star*. In a way, he says, it was "the happiest time of my life." He started at the bottom, writing obituaries and weather reports. Before he left, six months later, he wrote a three-part series which won him the Arizona Press Club's award for the year's best religious feature. He enjoyed the hours and the secular atmosphere, but "the strange tug of the ministry" pulled him away, and his denomination's Board of American Missions soon set him to work organizing a new church in Tucson. From then until the end of 1966, he was first mission developer and then pastor of Dove of Peace Lutheran Church. During the last two of those years, he was moderator of *Encounter*, a weekly local interfaith television program which kept him regularly in contact with Catholics, Jews, a variety of Protestants and many people of no church affiliation.

Over the years, Robert M. Herhold has become well known within the Lutheran Church in America and in more broadly ecumenical circles. In January, 1967, he accepted an appointment as associate director of the Commission on the Church and Race of the Southern California Council of Churches and was a liaison person with community organizations in Watts and other parts of Los Angeles. He soon discovered that the best thing a concerned white person can do today is to try to do something about white racism. Eight months later he became pastor of First Lutheran Church in Palo Alto. By this time, he had accumulated a considerable fund of short writings, and he put some of them together and sent them to me. Since I had edited Malcolm Boyd's *Are You Running With Me, Jesus?* he wondered if I might be interested in a book of these. These what? I had never seen anything quite like them—just as I had never seen anything quite like Malcolm Boyd's prayers. But they touched the same editorial instinct, with their freshness, their honesty, their blend of humor and insight. When I showed them to my friend Victor Weybright, his response was one of instant delight, and he agreed to publish such a book.

Funny, You Don't Look Christian—the title itself struck the first spark, but the idea underlying it followed through with warmth and insight. Many a reader, I suspect, will find much more in this book than he thought on first sight. For beyond the wit of this and other titles within the book are very real and very human people of all kinds. All the kinds a minister meets—and some the average minister may not. It is a very human book. But like Malcolm Boyd's best seller, its deepest reality, its deepest humanity, puts us in touch with ultimate questions and values. Some will recognize in it the image and spirit of God; others may choose a different vocabulary. To me, the book eludes the usual pigeonholes of orthodoxy and liberalism—perhaps because it combines elements of both with the secular accent with which Christians today must speak if they are to speak meaningfully.

All of these pieces are drawn from life. A few are autobiographical. They are in the style of the secular city, articulating the ways in which man experiences his basic needs in the world of here and now. Herhold's observations are drawn from life as we live it, casual and vernacular; but his concern for the things that really matter—for what concerns God—is firm and solid. After the smile comes reflection, for there is spiritual sustenance to be found here, even if (or perhaps because) it doesn't always *look* Christian.

The church and its ministry are, as we all know, far from what they should be. Bob Herhold is among their severest critics—and so am I. We recognize that the church and its people are a good deal less than sacred. We are not alone in thinking this way; nor are we alone in sensing that a positive note must be sounded as well. Perhaps the most hopeful portent for Christianity today is precisely the ambivalence many of us feel about the future of organized religion. If it is to be saved, it must be for some higher purpose than its complacent self-perpetuation. Some of us have already departed, without abandoning faith. Pastor Herhold, from within, says: "I have a lover's quarrel with the church, and I suspect I shall never get over it." The church needs such men; without them it has no savor. And it is the tang of leavening which matters most. If the church has any future, it will be because men like Robert M. Herhold remain inside it. If it has none, it will be because it turns a deaf ear to such voices as his, regardless of appearances. But to paraphrase the Apostle Paul, whether we are in or out of the church, whether we look Christian or not, we are the Lord's. Bob Herhold, with this book, has found more entertaining ways to say that very thing—not by scolding, not by sermonic vehemence, but through parables and vignettes that mirror our lives. That, it seems to me, is the best way of preaching the gospel—as one urban human being to another. For, come to think of it, dear reader, it's funny, but *you* may not look Christian either. Or if you do, this may be just the book to deepen your understanding into what's for real. Either way, you will find it worth reading again and again. If you can resist quoting from it to friends, I shall be very much surprised.